HOME
BY
NOW

HOME
BY
NOW

MEG KEARNEY

FOUR WAY BOOKS

TRIBECA

Editorial Office
Four Way Books
POB 535, Village Station
New York, NY 10014
www.fourwaybooks.com

Library of Congress Cataloging-in-Publication Data
Kearney, Meg.
Home By Now / Meg Kearney.
p. cm.— (A Malcolm McDonald Series Selection)
ISBN 978-1-884800-94-8 (pbk. : acid-free paper)
I. Title.
PS3611.E2H66 2009
811'.6—dc22
2009004714
ISBN-13: 978-1-884800-94-8

This book is manufactured in the United States of America
and printed on acid-free paper.

Four Way Books is a not-for-profit literary press. We are grateful for the
assistance we receive from individual donors, public arts agencies,
and private foundations.

This publication is made possible with public funds
from the National Endowment for the Arts
and from the New York State Council on the Arts, a state agency.

Distributed by University Press of New England
One Court Street, Lebanon, NH 03766

We are a proud member of the Council of Literary Magazines and Presses.

[clmp]

for Joseph Sheehan Patrick Kearney (1921 – 1990)

TABLE OF CONTENTS

HOME BY NOW

AMONG THE MISSING

CARNAL

I suppose squirrels have their hungers, too,
like the one I saw today with the ass end of a mouse
jutting from its mouth. I was in the park;
I'd followed the stare of a dog, marveled
as the dog seemed to marvel that the squirrel
didn't gag on the head, gulped so far down
the squirrel's throat nearly all that was visible
was the grey mouse rump, its tail a string
too short to be saved. The dog and I couldn't
stop gawking. The squirrel looked stunned himself—
the way my ex, The Big Game Hunter, looked
when I told him I was now a vegetarian.
We'd run into each other at a street fair
in Poughkeepsie. The hotdog he was eating
froze in his hand, pointed like a stubby finger,
accused me of everything I'd thought
I'd wanted, and what I'd killed to get it.

"HOLD FAST"
—the motto of clan MacLeod, Isle of Skye, Scotland

Inside Dunvegan, the clan MacLeod Castle
still reigning over Scotland's scraggly shore,
beyond the roped-off tapestries and glass-
encased kilts, past pewter goblets and family
portraits (more kilts, a legacy of mutton-chops),
narrow steps twist down to a hall that leads
to what had been the kitchen; and in the other
dank direction, the dungeon's ghastly pit.
Cuisine being what it was in the 14th century
(wild boar, deer, the odd cabbage), cooks' tools
strung above a caldron appear fit for their task:

a dozen unnerving knives, the handy ax, a wooden
ladle that might also serve as shovel or varmint-
whacker. No one knows which devilish ancestor
devised the dungeon next door, its vented wall
an abuse of aromas—seasoned stews, baking
bread, venison roast. Shivering on his slab
of stone, the prisoner must have dreamed
of his wife, her dark eyes' flash as she turned
from the evening fire, steam veiling her face
as she set the bowl before him. She'd wait
for him to lift the spoon, for his nod

of pleasure before she sat down beside him.
If only he'd been content with that first bird
he'd poached. He was nearly to the forest's
edge, nearly home free when that second

4

pheasant stirred the bush, preening like a queen
in her dappled robes—oh, he could not say
No. And coughing in his cell, he knew that love,
like hunger, is a covetous ache for a feast just
out of reach. Yet, what he'd stolen sustained him:
memory of her downy breast, and her body's oil,
a balm still seeping into his hands.

CONCEPTION, AMERICAN STYLE

I.

I'm a lady's man I'm a cherry intact
I'm pulling into the rest stop
            unbuttoning my blouse
I'm twelfth-hour whiskers
I am tongue I am breast
I'm pussy throb and neck aflame
I'm zipper and the other zipper
I'm steaming all the windows
I'm delirious radio, stockings run amok
I'm finger, hand, a nipple, another
I'm breath and I'm muscle
            again, again
I am salt
I am musk
I am slap-it wet
I am murk and egg and the fish shoving my head in
I am already dividing I'm multiplying
            oh pious mother, oh charming father.

II.

They've returned to the parking lot: dim light reveals
a sheen of sweat on her forehead and upper lip.
Her Scottish skin is blotchy, as if she'd had a drink.

He lights her cigarette, regards her in the match
glow, while her eyes linger on a tuft of hair—
she'd kissed him there—at his shirt's open collar.

She is trembling; it's time for her to go.
They stand by the car and he takes her hand,
kisses it; she presses her other hand to her heart.

Then they notice her blouse, something askew—
she mismatched the buttons, and
they laugh. It was her first time. She thinks

he has made her a promise. He must have
known that. He leans, kisses her. Wherever,
whoever he is, he must have known that much.

FUNDEVOGEL

"Fundevogel, do not forsake me,
and I will never forsake you."
—from the Brothers Grimm

Perhaps father is another word
for sleep. My dead father sleeps
without rest, crossing between

this life and the last. My blood
father sleeps in Florida, or
Budapest, or anywhere I am not.

In his sleep my dead father glides
through the window. He is young
again; I sit on his lap while he reads

The Frog Prince and *Fundevogel*,
the foundling baby carried away
by a bird. In his world, my dead

father reads the Brothers Grimm.
We dream up a happy ending.
In Boca Raton, my blood father

dreams, feverish, grinding his teeth,
murmuring a story that his wife,
propped on her elbow in bed,

has strained for years to catch.
Watching him, she knows
the dream is about to end:

he twitches, swallows, says, Come
back. But the woman and the little girl
wander hand-in-hand into the forest.

He opens his mouth, closes it.
He doesn't know their names.
This is where the story ends.

He wakes. My dead father goes
gray in my room, closes
his book, kisses my forehead.

Margaret, he says, it's time to sleep. But
Father, what to do about this meddlesome
crow, pecking at my window?

SEPTEMBER 12, 2001: VIEW OF DOWNTOWN MANHATTAN FROM MY BEDROOM WINDOW

The amputee insists
her legs are still
down there

She feels them
burning—
She knows

when the smoke clears
they will be
standing

INSTEAD OF GOING STRAIGHT
TO THE DANCING BEAR INN

East Glacier Park, Montana

After burgers at Two Medicine we head to the saloon:
six wooden stools with cracked leather seats, a rough-
hewn table near the dart board in the back. Johnny
Cash smolders through the smoke. She wants whiskey,

asks for rye, but all they have is bourbon
and an eye for women dumb enough to step into a bar
with no windows and a plywood door. It could be 1978,
not 2004—we could be in my parents' basement,

after my brother strung the chili-pepper lights and raised
the floor. We'd pass around the reefer and chug warm
beer, then trudge up the hatchway stairs to piss. I tell her
this while the Glacier boys rise around us like a flood.

One with his eye on her wants to know where we're
from. "East," she says, as I slip her her purse. We leave
our stools twirling, slink out to the street. Our hair stinks
in this mile-high air. She says, "We'll always be

alone." A star spits across the sky, then it's gone. We swear
we'll never go back there. Meanwhile, the cowboys inside
ride the guy we just ditched. "Goddamn flirts!" he shouts,
then turns back to the boys as they slug 'n smoke 'n curse.

VIRGIN

In the playground of idle minds
I'm riding a blue bicycle.
My girlfriend waits behind

the jungle gym, mixing orange
juice and Seagram's sloe gin.
This is how we learn to be

sixteen: cotton-candy liquor
and a smoke on the slide. We
radiate patchouli and musk;

compare our breasts; share this
secret cocktail while our tongues
turn to grenadine, syrupy with

boys. My bike cuts a figure-
eight sexy enough to catch
the Devil's eye. Now here he is,

shinnying up the monkey bars and
he wants *me*. Just like I'd imagined.
Just like mother promised.

FIRST BLOW JOB

Suddenly I knew what it was to be my uncle's Labrador retriever,
young pup paddling furiously back across the pond with the prized
duck in her mouth, doing the best she could to keep her nose in the air

so she could breathe. She was learning not to bite, to hold the duck
just firmly enough, to command its slick length without leaving marks.
She was about to discover that if she reached the shore, delivered this

duck just the way she'd been trained, then Master would pet her head
and make those cooing sounds; maybe later he'd let her ride
in the cab of the truck. She would rest her chin on his thigh all the way

home, and if she had been good enough, she might get to wear
the rhinestone-studded collar, he might give her a cookie, he might
not shove her off the bed when he was tired and it was time for sleep.

FOR DEAR LIFE

We did not wake my mother from her naps. We just
didn't. But that day, when Mrs. Reuter held my right
arm in her tanned tennis grip, I knew what I had to do
and she could not keep me from it. She thought I wanted
my father—to go to him, sprawled and bleeding from
his mouth and nose into Keller's summer-brown lawn—
but I pulled free and surprised her, dashing past Dad,
past the bicycle still in the road and twisted like his face,
past his glasses, silver frames smashed into a squint,
glass spit and sparkling in the gravel, through Moershell's
yard and Strickland's, past the can we kids kicked every
night before suppertime, then into our own driveway,
around the garage to the backyard where my mother
lay snoring softly in the hammock, arms folded across
her flat belly, skin scented with Jean Naté and Scotch,
and I did not hesitate, I snatched her hands in mine
and shook them, shouting, Wake up, Mom, wake up.

MATERNAL

The farmer who keeps his cows in this field
arrives with a truck stacked with hay.
"Here you go!" he shouts, tossing a bale over

the fence. He mimics their lowing with his dinner
bellow, and the cows canter toward him—
what a chorus of moos! Our neighbors used to

keep a milk cow on their little farm, called her
Slingshot for the way she'd burst
from the barn. My mother painted a picture

of that barn, but left the animals out—
she was good with people but didn't trust
her hand with cows, or those nasty chickens

that pecked our shins when Mr. Ryan let us
in to gather eggs. One Halloween, Margaret
and I stole some brown ones, eggs warm as shit,

to throw at Oliver Sandberg's house. He once
said he wanted to be Hitler when he grew up, but
we knew Oliver had Hitler confused with

Houdini. "Dumb as a stone, that one,"
the farmer says of the speckled calf
snuffling stale white bread out of his

hand. Oliver was a damn good magician for a fifth grader. Once made a whole chicken disappear, and claimed his parents were next.

He scared the bejesus out of us. "This one here's gonna taste real sweet," says the farmer. "I'm the only mother she's ever known."

1970

When I got my head stuck between the porch rails
I didn't know enough yet to hate my body, but I knew
a thing or two about smoking my father's cigars
with Patrick Dunn under the pines behind his house,

and puking while my brother rolled joints and stacked
45s on the record player in his room. My sister
turned me on to Carole King and JT, swore her friends
would die in Vietnam because her peace medallion

was flammable. She tried to teach me to dance, but
I was never graceful—it wasn't a surprise,
me wedged in that railing. How did they get me out?
Nixon was president; Martin Luther King

was dead. The whole country was in a fix,
my father said, though he never said a word
about the cigars. His heart was a shooting star;
I thought he could fix everything. My mother

believed she could fix his failing heart with home-
made tomato sauce and a Manhattan on the rocks.
My mother rose with the fish; she was unable to
cry; she put her hand to my father's cheek, then went

back to work. Uncle Frank called her a good German:
Arbeit Macht Frei, he said, and she nearly kicked him
in the shins. I loved Uncle Frank, but I don't want to
talk about him. Uncle Frank's dead. But let's say I do

remember how they got my head out of that railing.
It took a crowbar—took what seemed forever
because the adults had their loads on by then. That
night my best friend and I took turns wearing the wig

and high heels: we were knobby-knee glamorous, we
were nothing like our parents. Uncle Frank leaned
in the doorframe as we preened, fluttered, eyed
the dapper men, toasted each other with empty glasses.

RESCUED

I have been among the missing, clanging
my rusted rattle in the nursery rubble.

I have been among the foundlings, poster
child for Catholic charity. They sorted us

like laundry, separated coloreds from
whites, and if there was any doubt about

a baby's blood she was whisked cross-
town to a freelance anthropologist.

Though my heart wheezed like a bagpipe, I was
saved by my skin: illegitimate but convent

white. I thank God for that, and for the man
who gave me his name. Do you blame me?

I admit it: I did not look back. I couldn't save
the others. I batted my big brown eyes at that

man and his barren wife—my first act
of seduction—and promised to be a good girl.

LIVING IN THE VOLCANO

All I want is a falafel, a macramé purse,
and First Piccolo in the marching band.

Hey, my sunless tan puts an orange slant
on everything I say. I mean I want to *be*

first, and hippie free … but my tongue
is a branding iron shaped in an "X"

(I kiss your eyes and you're dead), First
Trombone turns left at the 40, and

the rest of us wave bye-bye, too grumpy
to follow. We say, Let's practice more, earn

this pride of prima donnas a scholarship
to Party University. We say, Let's melt

down the horns, buy us some brewskies
and vitamin M. We need to forget, for a two-

day bender, how much we can't stand
ourselves. But this is high school. And now

Mother, our First Fan, has skipped town
with the bake sale money and Finnegan,

our only tuba. Who needs TV drama? This
is life in the volcano. This is as cold as it gets.

SOCKS

My father's body has ceased to shock me.
His skin runs over his bones like a slow
river, rippling where belly meets hip. We've
learned how to hold him: one arm each around
his back, one hand under each thigh; Mom
and I stand on opposite sides of his
bed and, on the count of three, lift him
onto the bedpan. We close our eyes—
Dad, then me. Oh, he pants, it's so damn cold
as I tell myself, *I am not the first
daughter to do this.* Afterward, Mom pulls
his gown down over the stones of his hips
while I train my eyes on the Gold Toe socks
I'll later steal, when Mom gives away his suits.

STUBBORN

My sister and I take turns shaving his face.
We're terrified we'll cut him; his blood's
thinner than the soup at school. I'm better
with his right cheek, she with his left, and as
we work he teases me, *I knew there was some
purpose for lefties in this world.* Watch out,
I say, or I'll let the night nurse do this,
and he gives my sister a wink. *My wife
and daughters are like bulldogs
on a meat wagon,* he tells the nurses.
Even after I'm dead, they won't let go.

THE WAIT

Somewhere down that hallway three surgeons
have sliced my father from thorax to abdomen,
spread his ribs like the hull of a ship, and lifted

out his heart. A pump will do his heart's work
while the surgeons work on his heart and we do
what families in waiting rooms do: we pace—

from chair to water fountain to hall, desperate
to see a surgeon there with a hopeful look
on his face. One of them, shuffling down

the corridor in his green smock and booties,
updates us every few hours. None of the news
has been cheerful. *It does no good to worry,*

Dad said this morning. *It's in God's hands.*
His speech was slightly slurred. They'd already
given him the first shot. All four of us stood in line

to kiss his cheek, my mother last. She whispered
her love in his ear, then said, *See you in a few
hours.* It's September, and by now she's down

to ninety-nine pounds, maybe. She never seems
to sleep, never needs the bathroom. Over the course
of seventeen and a half hours I discover

my brother drinks coffee with milk; my sister
has switched to tea. Trips to the cafeteria break
the vigil, but I'm riddled with worry

I'll miss something. We're good at this,
well-practiced in the art of the wait, devoted
to its hermetic rituals, inside jokes. I've planted

myself as sentinel at the door where the waiting
room meets the hall. I count ceiling tiles
and then the dots inside them—when I squint

my eyes, they come at me 3-D. We are exploring
the bottoms of our pocketbooks, thumb wrestling,
staring at magazines when the men in green finally

appear. All three of them this time. We huddle
like a team. *It's over,* says the one wearing glasses—
I'm sorry. My mother faints. He catches her.

DANNY BOY: MY FATHER'S FUNERAL

The casket is open
during the wake's first

hour for "private family
viewing." Bill, the funeral

director, tries to take my
hand. *Don't make her,*

my sister says. I have
been in the bathroom,

puking. When the casket
is shut, I am a dutiful

daughter, stand for hours
saying, *Thanks for coming*

to the blur of faces stretching
out the door and down

the sidewalk. All night
we eat nothing but

orchids and lilies. My mother
cannot cry. Bill brings us

aspirin, keeps our water
cups full, keeps tapes of Irish

ballads rolling. I barely hear
my brother: *"The pipes,*

the pipes are calling..."
I've never heard him sing.

I hate this song, he says.

SO THIS GRASSHOPPER WALKS INTO A BAR

HOUSE FOR SALE

after the divorce: for P.W.

I buried Saint Joseph headfirst
in the yard. Anointed with perfume,
wrapped in an old handkerchief,

he must have heard my supplications
as I dug the hole, lowered him down,
packed the dirt, begged forgiveness.

Victim of faith or superstition,
Saint Joseph bears the indignity
of mud, the vulgarity of worms,

but this house will not sell. The realtor
flashes his wily grin at the next
newlywed couple; suggests, arching

one eyebrow, the potential
of the spare bedroom. I hide
in my car praying to Saint Joseph

to let some other woman stuff peppers
at the kitchen counter; let that
woman cry out, for whatever reason,

in the bedroom. I even wish her joy
here: garden flowers on the sill,
birthday cake cooling on a rack,

a man in the backyard, building
a swing set. Just make her want this
house, please. Let me dig up

my plastic saint, snap the mud
from his little blanket, and ditch this ring
where dogs are sure to piss.

RUM & COKE & A NEW APARTMENT

She knew herself well enough to say
no to a place that shared a parking lot

with a bar. She knew, scribbling the deposit
check, that the yellow halogen mounted right

there on its pole meant her bedroom would never
be dark; that The Pirate, stoned and grinning

neon above the bar's front door, would lure
her like a siren to a stool that swiveled and rum

on the rocks, a splash of coke, no lemon—just
another night of bullshitting about the rain

and a book she planned to write when she had enough
time. Funny how people always find shelter

talking about the weather. Her dash
from the apartment door through the rain

to the bar that first night gave her entrance
a sheen of innocence—water dripping

from her hair—she was a girl seeking
refuge, not a woman slinking into a bar

alone. It was a part she could play, and the men
let her, one giving up his seat and his cozy

jacket, another shouting "Richie! Give this lady
a drink." "Richie," she murmured, "the usual."

The men chortled. Richie winked.
She was practically a regular already.

NATURE POETRY

for William Matthews

Bill hated the separation implied by the term. "What's *this?*"
he'd ask, gesturing toward what lay beyond our classroom
window. From "NAC" 6-303 in Harlem, Manhattan blinked
and glowed like a floor of stalagmite, lit by its own desire
to exist. What was it? Concrete, glass, steel—meaning
limestone, silica, gypsum, sand, manganese, sodium,
sulfur, ore—anything unnatural here? Here, in the city,
we steel ourselves against the elements—steel, from
the Old High German *stak*, "to resist"—and we fight
like the animals we are for our own little plots of privacy
amidst all this concrete (from the Latin, *concret-us*,
past participle of *con-crescere*, "to grow together").
We're too much together, and all the while we make
like Adam and put names to things, just to say *This is
real, I exist in this world.* So we say "boulevard,"
"taxi," "skyscraper," "villain"—which used to mean
you worked on a farm, but now means you better
have eyes in the back of your head when you walk
down the boulevard. "Be careful going home,"
Bill would say at the end of class. "It's a jungle
out there." Yes, we'd agree. Naturally.

IN THE DAYS OF CODE ORANGE

Terrorists might take the Empire State
Building next, might take you or me or
the red eye to L.A. Our fears escalate
like the news anchor's tits: we're not sure
if they're real or not. The men in black
keep such secrets, secured in the public's

interest; yet they're never hung up by facts.
Meanwhile, a woman dies cold in the park.
An underemployed chef is driving a cab.
A foster mother starves the boys in her care.
The anthrax assassin sits tight in his lab.
They'd drill Ground Zero, if oil were there.

Love, let's live by a code the color of wine.
We have this cup, and so little time.

THE PRODIGAL FATHER

It's too late—he can't go back, can't gas up the old Ford
Fairlane and head for Midland Avenue, for frosted mugs
and football at Sullivan's or buckets of beer with all
the Smiths and McErlanes down at Sandy Point
Beach. No more Scotch and tube steaks at the King's

Park drive-in, no more Everly Brothers and Elvis and his
hands on a girl's hips in the smoky dim of Shady's
or the Golden Nugget. *You're my piece of gold,*
he purred into that last girl's ear. *Hell, I must be
at the rainbow's end.* And the way she looked at him—

well, he doesn't want to think about her or what
he said later in the Fairlane's back seat. She should
have known better—she was one of those nice
girls—as he knew better than to call, or be seen
in the Nugget for a while, though soon he'd heard

she'd moved, maybe Arizona, maybe New Mexico.
It took nine or ten pints at Sullivan's to convince
himself that the rest of that rumor wasn't true—
or if it was, she could have been knocked up
by anybody. Another couple of pints and he knew

he was moving too, taking the wife and kids north
to New England, to a new life. But it took more
than a shot of whiskey to silence that song, that
wordless ballad troubling his head, something
with a fiddle, something with a pipe, a mandolin.

SO THIS GRASSHOPPER WALKS INTO A BAR

The trick is to pay close attention to that vodka
you're pouring, and lie: Nope, haven't heard
that one. Then grab the OJ, glance out toward
the pool table to see if Phil's watching you

as PJ or Tin-Knocker Sam says, "And the grasshopper
hops onto the stool…." Linda sees you're on edge.
She's on her fourth pint since 7:15. You like her, start
to wonder if she'll cut herself off when the bartender

in the joke says, "We've got a drink named after you!"
"One for the road?" asks Linda. You check your watch.
It's only nine o'clock, and already the smoke eater's
snapping like a wet towel. Already there's a line

of quarters shining like Mary Mack's buttons
down one side of the pool table's faux mahogany
bumper and there's Phil, shouting, "Rack 'em!"
"One more," you relent. Sam says he's buying.

Sam's still waiting for his quarters to come up;
you were about to tell the Valley Girl joke but now
he's telling you how Son of Sam worked sheet metal,
too, and sad thing is he thinks he's flirting.

It's Friday and you've got a full bar, three-deep
and every seat taken, the five Miller brothers filling
the corner by the jukebox, singing along to "Take
It Easy" and waving for another round of ponies.

It's Miller they want, what else, and because Richie
didn't fill the cooler last night you've got to run
back to the walk-in for a bottle of Rosie's and a case.
Ed offers to help, as he always does, but you haul

your own behind the bar unless a keg kicks. You rest
a moment in the cooler's forty degrees, your breath
a trail of smoke. The rubber mat's a bit slick. Each time
you come here you're struck by how the cigarette reek

in your hair mixes with the musk in your turtleneck
and it doesn't smell bad. You're reminded of that
short story where the guy sticks his dead mother
in a restaurant freezer, remember how Mark kissed you

here the night before his wedding, how his glasses
frosted over, how he tasted like bourbon and fear.
Lugging out that case you know the local boys think
you're tough—yeah, you can fake it as well as Linda

can fake she's sober—that is, up to a point. Now
Phil's out by the pool table slinging cusses at some Vassar
boy, something about calling a shot. Phil can never
know about Mark—it was just that once. Shit,

he'd kill you. How many has *he* had so far tonight?
You eye the baseball bat between the trash can and keg
of Michelob, glad the Millers are still bangin' those
bottles, yuckin' it up through Cindy Lauper, waiting

for the next Eagles tune to come up. The boys have
backed you before. They won't mess with Phil—
it's an unspoken fact he's your man—but they can escort
out the college kid if things get ugly. Your head's

humming. You're gulping Diet Coke, regretting the line
you did off Cathy's finger in the ladies'. You call
"Goodnight" to Mr. Dugan, hoping a fight doesn't ruin
your shift or your chances for a decent tip from whoever

wins the table. You watch Mr. D sway in some
unseen wind as he reaches for the door. Thank God
he's walking home. You'll walk home, too, after
you lock up, but that's a jukebox of songs and a stockpile

of jokes from now. That's after the pool table's gone
quiet, like water when kids are through swimming,
after the cues are stowed in the umbrella stand, after
the Miller brothers have harmonized "Desperado."

You'll cash out, slam a shot, pour the tip jar into your
purse, elbow the light switch, turn the key in the door
and set the alarm. You'll step lightly across the parking
lot, past Phil's truck and Phil passed out at the wheel,

knowing he's been here waiting for you. You'd hoped
he'd gone home. He doesn't think you're a tough
girl. He thinks you're his, and you flirt too much
behind that bar. He thinks he knows what love is,

and as soon as he wakes he's gonna come pounding
on your door to prove it. And though like a bad joke
you've heard before, you know what's coming next,
you'll rise from bed, unbolt the door, and let him in.

GEORGE SAYS STOP WRITING ABOUT YOURSELF

New York, December 2001

This one's for George, who urged take off those
shit-kicker boots, leave your husband wrapped
in the scroll of last night's sheets, forget your mother
sipping a cigarette, a Dugan's Dew—forget
your other mother, your other father, too,

and the one you last saw in a coffin not looking
at all like himself, so much not-him you couldn't
bear be near that body. Forget your first kiss—
how it sounded like peanut butter, tasted like
a train. Stop talking about the Alabama Slammers

and four Blue Whales or those men you drove crazy
with your push-him, pull-him love. And don't speak
of babies, about not having them or the ugly one
who's so much a part of your nights she must be
real, her mongrel face breaking into sadness.

Don't talk about holding her above your head,
calling her Sweet Girl, Mama's Girl—how she almost
smiles. Just for George, this poem looks beyond
Sea Monkeys and that first Louisville Slugger.
It opens the window to the stench, three months

now of that smell, man-made, human, wafting
from downtown. This poem is in the street,
where war does its thing. See, there's a man
walking up Broadway: his shoes, suit, eyelashes,
lips covered with dust that used to be a building.

MITZVAH ON SATURDAY MORNING

You're on East 14th Street headed west
to buy a new seat for your bicycle.
In Casper, Wyoming, a hospice nurse
backs her car out of your parents'
driveway. Your father calls out

from his bed. What would you
have done if you'd caught the thief,
wrench in one hand, seat in the other?
Lorraine! your father calls again.
You would've taught the guy

another use for that wrench.
Your mother carries a plate, a cup
of water. Here I am, she sings, entering
the bedroom. Last month someone
stole the bell from your handle bars.

Your mother cuts a muffin in half.
Maybe a new bell, too, you think.
Last year, when your father could
still walk, they took the whole bike.
Try to eat it all, your mother says,

tucking a napkin under his chin.
You wait for the light to change
at First Avenue. What next? Exhaust
from a passing bus, roasted cashews.
This muffin tastes like dirt, your father

says. He takes another bite.
The bike-shop bag goes scrish-scrish
against your leg as you head home,
slip into Sloan's for extra-sharp
cheddar and a six-pack of Corona.

Your father's hand trembles, reaching
for the water glass. All morning
he watched a show about polar bears,
then switched to the weather channel.
A woman at the supermarket

check-out insists, These are the Concord
grapes. These grapes aren't organic.
Polar bears eat penguins! your father says.
Your mother is in the den. She holds
a book but really she is napping. Now

the woman with the grapes is in a tizzy:
her necklace has burst; it's raining silver
charms. It's raining in Denver,
your father says. You scan the floor
for small, shiny objects. It's fifty-five

in New York, calls your father. Your mother
is in the kitchen now, counting pills.
Here's something strange: a stone trinket,
an evil eye. You fear the woman might
hug you as you hand it to her. Lorraine,

your father says, I'm too tired to play my
flute. You wonder if it was bad luck to touch
that thing. Do you know the Hebrew word
for "good deed?" asks the woman. Your
father's face is angelic in the TV light.

AUBADE

Dulce, the piano begins: a kitchen
where an old woman sits in
the dark, glow of her cigarette's eye
lifting and dipping with the sigh
of a violin string. Soon the sun
is rising says the piano in a warm
run, like the steam from her cup
of tea. A second violin interrupts
to reveal a letter opened hours
ago in silence. It lies beside her
glasses, folded like a body. Years ago
she loved this time of day. The piano
remembers his blue cup; violins long
to see it there and pour a morning song.

HOME BY NOW

NEW HAMPSHIRE, LATE WINTER (2006)

Such a change of view—no World
Trade Center (that's a fact)—but
no Woolworth Building, either, no
twelve-story brick buildings flanking
my own and another crop across
the oval, where a thousand kids'
boot prints are mud. There, plane

trees, dirty white, echo what's left
of city snow. Here, snow slips off
the roof, portending the rain
Mount Washington forecasters said
would kill off winter faster than that
fisher cat snapped up the neighbor's
tabby. "Fisher cat can tear the head

off a horse," says Ken of Ken's Home
Appliances, Videos, Guns & Shooting
Range. Though this fabulous claim
might have been for our city-folk
benefit, we're street-smart and wary
enough not to let our Lab run the woods
at night alone. Which brings me

back to this view: those tree tops,
dull and leafless against
the cement-grey sky, are nearly all

that's visible from our upstairs
window—maples, oak, the dog's
tripod prints through the mushy
meadow. But from woods beyond

our woods, the crack-boom
of rifle fire: gunpowder, taste
of smoke and downtown
burning. The dog jerks awake.
BOOM. This view's no solace—
all those city hues, and below,
a drop of cardinal in the snow.

TATTOO

This is my bastard's birthmark
three ravens, leg to talon
this is the locket I kept in the dark
now an indelible totem

three ravens, leg to talon
heads and tails a hubless wheel
now an indelible totem
coat of arms, the family seal

heads and tails a hubless wheel
a right withheld since I was born
coat of arms, the family seal
now tattooed upon my arm

a right withheld since I was born
stranger who kept me in her womb
now tattooed upon my arm
act of contrition, my bruise, my wound

stranger who kept me in her womb
holds onto me and the one I call mother
act of contrition, my bruise, my wound
secret surrender that all of us cover

holds onto me and the one I call mother
who knows my blood isn't so simple
secret surrender that all of us cover
isn't absolved by a prodigal symbol

who knows my blood isn't so simple
as this, the baby I'd kept in the dark
secret surrender that all of us cover
this is my bastard's birthmark

POSTCARD FROM NEW HAMPSHIRE

to fellow raven mavens in New Jersey

I thought life here would be rife
with ravens—they'd be lined up
along the overhead wires
like black bikinis on a rack
at Macy's, daring me to bare
some, be *seen*—they'd make me feel
at home—but it's crows that shake me
at four a.m., rattling the bony branches
above the bat house in the dead maple
behind the shed. They're the country
version of car alarms, here
where not the drone of bees
but ATVs swell a summer
afternoon. I don't romanticize
country life, am no longer the kind
of poet to put words in the beaks
of birds. Winter's coming soon
and the closest I've come to raven
speak is a *New Yorker* cartoon.

DR. FRANKENSTEIN LEARNS
THE MOTHER HE NEVER MET IS DEAD

I hunted love with a bone saw,
a threaded needle between
my teeth. Scavenger of blood
and resemblance, I slaughtered
my siblings for body parts,
vowing, *We'll never be orphans
again.*
           Then I retreated
to a mother's dirty work:
sawing, stitching, scanning the sky
for lightning. My creation
was born to disappoint: she is so
unlovable. Now she's on the lam
again—shrieking, slobbering,
smashing everything.

ANEURYSM

Her artery, that snake,
swallowed a rat
decades ago. The rat
loved it so
inside the tunnel
of her body, it curled up
inside those walls, as rats
will do, and called
the tunnel home,
lounging there as if
it had found the dark
alley behind a bistro
bar—booze, cigarettes,
scraps of gourmet fare.
Burrowed in his trove
of trash, dozy from naps
and the muffling thrum—
no wonder that rat
never budged. Now
it's grown so fat
it couldn't scurry
if it felt the urge,
and the walls of that snake's
body have worn
thin, stretched with the bulge
turning into stone.
The only option: the rat's

abode has got to go,
says the surgeon, while
the rat lies low, smoking
a Virginia Slim, contemplating
home, the knife, the burst
of light.

COUNTRY SUMMER BLUES

Something small and brown is nesting in the blue-
bird's box. The dog won't cool
himself in the plastic pool, even though

we showed him how. Jays picked all the raspberries so
we don't have to. One red leaf: cruel
forecaster. What we thought were asters: meadow rue.

Three dry weeks seared the summer snow and new
wonder. Neighbors warn we're fools
to plant purple lilacs where the wood pile should go.

We watch out for ticks and the sheriff who's
nicknamed "the Nazi." We stick to the rules
and nod when we see him, as country folk do.

ON LEARNING THAT HENRY FORD
WAS AN ANTI-SEMITE

Now I am ashamed I bought that pickup truck
brand-new off the lot in 1989, and a custom cap
to match the F-150 Supercab, alpine green with chestnut
trim. She saved my life, "Large Marge," when I fell
asleep and took out a tamarack and stone wall. She kept
me dry in Shenandoah when a creek swallowed my tent.
She never lost her nerve climbing Titusville's icy hill.
She carted a winter's worth of wood from Rhinebeck
to Germantown, a piano from Poughkeepsie to LaGrange,
and a paeon of poets—one stressed, three unstressed—
from the Kinsman to the Frost Place for readings, then back
for more booze. It wasn't a Dodge or a GM, but that truck
paid its dues. Did I say ashamed? I meant never again.

HOME BY NOW

New Hampshire air curls my hair like a child's
hand curls around a finger. "Children?" No,
we tell the realtor, but maybe a dog or two.
They'll bark at the mail car (Margaret's
Chevy Supreme) and chase the occasional
moose here in this place where doors are left
unlocked and it's Code Green from sun-up,
meaning go ahead and feel relieved—
the terrorists are back where you left them
on East 20th Street and Avenue C. In New York
we stocked our emergency packs with whistles
and duct tape. In New England, precautions take
a milder hue: don't say "pig" on a lobster boat
or paint the hull blue. Your friends in the city
say they'll miss but don't blame you—they
still cringe each time a plane's overhead,
one ear cocked for the other shoe.

NEW HAMPSHIRE, LATE WINTER II (2007)

All that's left of the hawk
that struck the upstairs

window is a smudge, a slick
of oil, smear of dander

hard to reach with a rag
or paper towel. He must have

thought his reflection a rival
(imagine, being that sure of

anything)—he was
his own worst enemy.

That's how it is with
America these days, too—

and hawks stay the course.
This hawk doesn't bleed, but

his head hangs slack to his
chest, as if in shame.

He's still warm when we carry
him to the woods. We don't

speak of suicide flights
into buildings—we lay

the bird on a rock. In the next
morning's breeze a few gray

tufts of down wave from the stone
like tattered flags.

ELEGY FOR THE UNKNOWN FATHER

Maybe there's a reason I was left
without a map to find you, why

the trail to your door has long gone
arctic. I've sat here nearly an hour

on the bench that marks the grave
of the man who raised me. I know

the way to this place, the back roads
south of the highway, the pothole

just before the iron gate. I know
its sparrows and withering lilies as well

as I knew the face of this father
walking in the door with an armful

of firewood or a fist of flowers. See
the groundskeeper give me a wave?

He knows me by name.
I have never needed you less.

LETTER FROM VAUVENARGUES

Horses have been talking to me
in my sleep. They carry me through
ponds thick with cold, prows of their
chests parting the water as we rush

to save a pregnant woman, unseen
but in danger. And every morning
I wake to a butterfly, a saffron eye
that winks, slowly, on a shutter

as weathered and blue as I feel
in these dreams. I rise, open the window
to release a fly, cold-drunk, buzz-
thropping itself against the glass,

and let in the scent of mint and roses,
the grumble of frogs in the garden, old
men squatting on the stone edge
of the reflecting pool. Beyond them,

three willows stand for Bill and Larry
and a poet I never knew. Before
brewing coffee I wander through olive
trees and lavender, follow the stone

path around the pool, rest my face
against a willow's bark, rough, cool,
my cheek against a dead man's cheek,
and the frogs hear me coming, splosh

in with the minnows and carp,
mammoth carp that skim the pond's
surface with their mouths open wide,
like a woman's sex—hungry,

dangerous, vulnerable. But that's
my own desire speaking, just as
my pregnancy dreams must signify
a kind of fullness I seldom truly feel.

You'd call it "happiness." Yes, it's
as elusive as that, but tangible as these
fish, orange and white bodies burgeoning
into the very ideal of themselves.

Or, it's like the willows, each standing
for a poet someone loved so much
she had to find a way to cling to them
as best she could, planting trees

as we, in our clinging, might read poems
to each other in the car or
at the kitchen table. I could say
the butterfly signifies something else—

stands for Laure-Anne or you or
yet another mother watching over
me; there can never be enough
of them. I could say the frogs are

my fathers, haggling over birthrights.
But none of this is exactly what
I mean. This poem, Bill would say,
wants to be a bottle of wine, but

right now it's only the photograph
of a vineyard. Do you remember
the winery we discovered in Sainte Serre?
We were lost on the other side

of Mont Sainte Victoire, bursting with joy
for a few replete hours that afternoon,
then I was in tears again at dinner.
You would remind me, as you always do,

that we must hold on to what we can,
and let the rest go. Hold on—that's what
those horses say at night, through
their heroic and terrible swimming.

NOTES & DEDICATIONS

"1970" includes the phrase *Arbeit Macht Frei*, a German phrase meaning "work makes (one) free." The slogan was placed at the entrances to a number of Nazi concentration camps.

"Aubade" was inspired by the music of composer Stephen Dankner and is dedicated to Trudy Kearney and Lorraine Fleming.

"Carnal" quotes a line by Donald Hall: "string too short to be saved."

"Instead of Going Straight to the Dancing Bear Inn" is for Patricia Henley.

"Letter from Vauvenargues" is for Deborah Smith Bernstein.

"Mitzvah on Saturday Morning" is for Mike Fleming.

"Postcard from New Hampshire" is for Joan and Peter Wood.

"Rescued": This poem's first line was inspired by Dan Chaon's collection of short stories, *Among the Missing*.

"Virgin" was letterpress-printed as a broadside by Wells College Press, Aurora, New York, in 2006; "Rescued" was printed as a broadside by Wells College Press in 2009.

ACKNOWLEDGMENTS

I am grateful to the editors of the following publications in which
several of these poems (some in earlier versions) first appeared:
*Agni, Bellevue Literary Review, Colored Chalk, Ellipsis, Free Lunch,
Lumina, Luna, Melic Review, Ploughshares, Poetry, Rattapallax,
The Recorder, The Same, The Sun, Two Rivers Review,* and *Witness.*

Thanks also to the editors and publishers of the following anthologies,
which featured poems found in this book:
Blues for Bill: A Tribute to William Matthews (Akron University
Press, 2005); *The Book of Irish-American Poets from the 18th Century
to the Present* (Notre Dame Press, 2006); *Cosmo Doogood's Urban
Almanac 2006; Kestrel 20th Anniversary Anthology* (2009);
Never Before: Poems About First Experiences (Four Way Books 2005);
Poetry in Performance #31 (City College of New York, 2003);
The Poets' Grimm: 20th Century Poems from Grimm Fairy Tales
(Story Line Press, 2003); *Shade 2006* (Four Way Books, 2006); and
Urban Nature: Poems About Wildlife in the City (Milkweed, 2000).

I am deeply indebted to Martha Rhodes, Laure-Anne Bosselaar,
Michael Fleming, Donald Hall, Steven Huff, Sally Ball,
Ryan Murphy, Deborah Smith Bernstein, George Drew,
Peter Wood, Kurt Brown, Cornelius Eady, Linda Pastan,
Norma Fox Mazer, Jacqueline Woodson, Kathi Aguero,
Bob Shacochis, Bruce Bennett, Carol Houck Smith,
Thom Ward, Jett & Shelley Whitehead, Angela Krajick, and
Margaret Dunn Pulido for their encouragement, editorial
assistance, and generous spirits. I am grateful to The Frost Place
in Franconia, New Hampshire, for years of support and
enlightenment; and to the Virginia Center for the Creative Arts,
where much of this book was born. Special thanks goes to
Mike Filan and his gorgeous paintings, which inspired a few of
the poems in this book. And thanks always to my family, who
know how difficult it can be to claim a poet as kin.

Meg Kearney is the author of the poetry collection
An Unkindness of Ravens and *The Secret of Me*, a novel in verse
for teens. Her picture book, *Trouper the Three-Legged Dog*, is
forthcoming from Scholastic. Her poetry has been featured on
Poetry Daily and Garrison Keillor's "A Writer's Almanac," and
in such publications as *Agni, The Gettysburg Review, Ploughshares,*
and *Poetry*, as well as in numerous anthologies. Director of the
Solstice Low-Residency M.F.A. in Creative Writing at Pine Manor
College and the Solstice Summer Writers' Conference, Meg was
associate director of the National Book Foundation for eleven years.
She also taught poetry at the New School University. A repeat
fellow at the Virginia Center for the Creative Arts, Meg has also
received fellowships from the New York Foundation for the Arts
and the New York Times. She is a past president of the Hudson
Valley Writers' Association of upstate New York. Meg was born
in Manhattan and currently resides in New Hampshire. For more
information, visit www.megkearney.com.